KU-252-055

Why Science Matters

Fighting Crime

TURRIFF ACADEMY
LIBRARY

Ian Graham

Heinemann
LIBRARY

www.heinemann.co.uk/library
Visit our website to find out more information about **Heinemann Library** books.

To order:
 Phone 44 (0) 1865 888066
 Send a fax to 44 (0) 1865 314091
Visit the Heinemann Bookshop at www.heinemann.co.uk/library to browse our catalogue and order online.

First published in Great Britain by Heinemann Library, Jordan Hill, Oxford OX2 8EJ, part of Pearson Education Limited, a company incorporated in England and Wales having its registered office at Edinburgh Gate, Harlow, Essex, CM20 2JE – Registered company number: 00872828

© Pearson Education Limited 2009
The moral right of the proprietor has been asserted.

All rights reserved. No part of this publication may be reproduced in any form or by any means (including photocopying or storing it in any medium by electronic means and whether or not transiently or incidentally to some other use of this publication) without the written permission of the copyright owner, except in accordance with the provisions of the Copyright, Designs and Patents Act 1988 or under the terms of a licence issued by the Copyright Licensing Agency, Saffron ——House, 6–10 Kirby Street, London EC1N 8TS (www.cla.co.uk). Applications for the copyright owner's written permission should be addressed to the publisher.

Editorial: Andrew Farrow, Megan Cotugno, and
              Harriet Milles
Design: Steven Mead
Illustrations: Gordon Hurden
Picture research: Ruth Blair
Production: Alison Parsons

Originated by Modern Age
Printed and bound in China by Leo Paper Products

ISBN 978 0 4310 4067 7
13 12 11 10 09
10 9 8 7 6 5 4 3 2 1

British Library Cataloguing-in-Publication data
Graham, Ian, 1953-
  Fighting crime. - (Why science matters)
  1. Forensic sciences - Juvenile literature
  I. Title
  363.2'5
A full catalogue record for this book is available from the British Library

Acknowledgements
The publisher would like to thank the following for permission to reproduce photographs:
©Alamy pp 11 (Mikael Karlsson), 30 (Andrew Lambert/Leslie Garland Picture Library); ©Corbis pp 24 (Ali Abbas/EPA), 32 & 33 (Lester V. Bergman), 13 (Richard Chung/Reuters), 21 (Mediscan), 10 (Nogues Alain/Corbis Sygma), 47 (Neal Preston), 25 (Evan Schnieder/EPA), 9 (Ramin Talaie); ©Foster & Freeman p 20; ©Getty Images pp5 (Metropolitan Police), 40 (C. Sherburne/PhotoLink), 31 (Natasja Weitsz); © Francisco de Goya, Dona Isabel de Porcel, The National Gallery p 42; ©PA Photos/AP p45; © Science Photo Library pp 14 (Biomedical Imaging Unit, Southampton General Hospital), 22, 34 & 35 (Michael Donne, University of Manchester), 6, 15, 26 & 36 (Mauro Fermariello), 12 (Peter Menzel), 19 (David Parker), 41 (Philippe Psaila), 8 (Paul Rapson), 29 (Dr Jurgen Scriba); 4 & 19 (Tek Image), 16 (Jim Varney), 23 (Charles D. Winters). Background images supplied by ©istockphoto

Cover image of computer artwork of a glowing handprint reproduced wth permission of © Science Photo Library/Pasieka and ©istockphoto.

The publishers would like to thank Andrew Solway for his invaluable assistance in the preparation of this book.

Every effort has been made to contact copyright holders of any material reproduced in this book. Any omissions will be rectified in subsequent printings if notice is given to the publishers.

Disclaimer
All the Internet addresses (URLs) given in this book were valid at the time of going to press. However, due to the dynamic nature of the Internet, some addresses may have changed, or sites may have ceased to exist since publication. While the author and publishers regret any inconvenience this may cause readers, no responsibility for any such changes can be accepted by either the author or the publishers.

Contents

Some words are printed in bold, **like this**. You can find out what they mean in the glossary.

Scene of crime

In the darkness of a moonless night, a car pulls up in front of a house. The driver gets out and hurries through rain to the front door. He does not see a figure crouching in the garden. As he opens the door, he's pushed inside from behind. He fights back. The two men struggle. The attacker's wet shoes slip on the floor leaving muddy footprints. A wall mirror shatters. Fragments of glass shower the attacker, cutting his hand. One of the figures falls to the ground, fatally injured. The attacker leaves, pressing blood-stained fingers on the door as he goes. No-one witnessed the crime or saw the killer's face. But the crime scene now contains all the information necessary to identify the killer ...

Someone heard the sound of fighting, and called the police. Their telephone call starts a chain of events that involves dozens of investigators and scientists. Police officers rush to the scene. People living nearby tell the officers they were woken by shouting, glass breaking, and footsteps running away. The first thing the officers do is to protect anyone in danger and call help for anyone who is injured. A doctor confirms that the person found at the scene is dead.

When a serious crime is committed, the crime scene is like a jumble of puzzle pieces. If investigators can find the right pieces and put them together in the right way, they may be able to find out what happened and who was responsible.

The officers inspect the crime scene without touching or moving anything. They try to preserve every piece of **evidence** that might identify the person or people who committed the crime. At this stage, no-one knows which piece of evidence will turn out to be the most important. It might be something obvious, like a blood stain, or it might be the tiniest trace of something that looks unimportant at first.

Security cameras may have recorded people or cars on their way to the crime scene or making their escape from it. Police officers seize the recordings.

Raising questions

Crime scene investigators arrive and begin to examine the scene. The clues they see raise questions in their minds. Where did that blood come from? Who made that shoe print? Why is that mirror broken? If there is a body at the scene, how did the person die and when? Talking to witnesses and **suspects** provides some of the answers, but science is often the key to filling in the blanks and learning the rest of the story.

It is vital to preserve the evidence at the crime scene. Only people who have a good reason to visit the crime scene are allowed in. A record is kept of who arrives and leaves, together with the times. The officers who work in the crime scene itself wear protective suits, face masks, gloves, and overshoes so that they do not contaminate the evidence with their own fingerprints, sweat, hair, or clothes fibres.

Searching for clues

Once investigators move in to search for evidence and remove it, the crime scene can not be put back to the way it was found. It is important to have a record of what the untouched crime scene looked like. The whole crime scene is photographed before a search begins. If the scene is a room in a house, the whole room is photographed, then parts of the room, then close-up photographs of tables, chairs, and individual items are taken. The scene may also be videoed. Next, investigators make a careful search for evidence. When anything of interest is found, its position is noted and it is photographed before being moved. A measuring scale, like a ruler, is placed next to each item to show its size.

A crime scene is photographed in detail so that there is a record of the position of every object before anything is moved.

THE SCIENCE YOU LEARN: SEARCH PATTERNS

The search for evidence at a crime scene must be done methodically so that nothing is missed. Crime investigation teams can use different methods when searching for evidence. One method is a *spiral* search, when the crime investigators start searching in the middle of the crime scene, and work outwards in a spiral. Another method is a *zone* search, where the investigating team divides a crime scene into zones. Each member of the team examines a zone. A third method is the *grid* search. The crime area is searched in parallel lines, that form a grid of squares (see the illustration below). A *line* search is better for a large expanse of open ground. A line of officers walk or crawl across the ground in parallel lines, looking for evidence. If a river or lake must be searched, police divers are brought in.

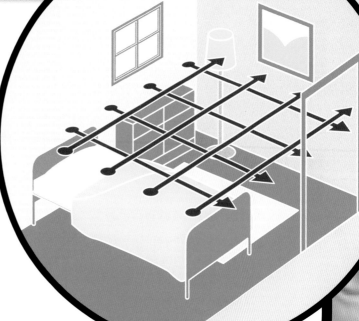

The grid search pattern

Collecting samples

Stains that might be blood are soaked up onto **swabs**. Strands of hair are picked up with tweezers. Hair and fibres are also collected by patting sticky tape onto a surface. When the tape is pulled away, loose hair and fibres come with it. Depending on the crime, electronic devices, such as computers and mobile phones, may be taken away.

Each piece of evidence is put into its own bag and sealed. Swabs are sealed in plastic tubes. Evidence bags and tubes are numbered and may also have barcodes. The sealed evidence containers should not be opened until they are inside a crime laboratory. A record is kept to show where all the evidence is and who is responsible for it at every moment. This is called the chain of custody. This record-keeping is vital to ensure that evidence is not tampered with.

Dusting a surface with fingerprint powder makes invisible fingerprints appear as if by magic. The powder is gently dusted onto the surface with a soft brush so that the print is not disturbed.

Invisible evidence

Crime scene investigators have to search for evidence that might not be visible. Anyone who touches something with bare hands leaves fingerprints behind. Fingerprints are patterns of lines made by the raised ridges on the fingertips. When a finger touches something, oily sweat on the fingertips is left behind in the shape of the raised ridges. Each person has their own unique fingerprint.

Fingerprints in smudges of dirt or blood are easy to see, but there may be other fingerprints that can't be seen. An invisible print is called a latent print. Making a latent print visible is called developing the print, but how do you find something that is invisible?

Places where fingerprints might have been left are examined with an **ultraviolet** lamp or a laser. Some of the substances in fingerprints glow under these lights. If prints are spotted, the surface is dusted with fine powder. The powder sticks to the prints and makes them easier to see.

Powder and glue

The most common fingerprint powder is aluminium. Other powders can be used if a print will not show up well with aluminium. Powder prints are lifted by putting clear sticky tape over them. When the tape is peeled back, the dusting powder print comes with it. The tape is then stuck down on a piece of card.

Powder is not very good for developing prints on paper or cloth. These surfaces soak up oily sweat, so there is nothing for the powder to stick to. Instead, the materials are taken back to the laboratory. There, they are treated with a chemical that reacts with fingerprints and changes their colour. Other difficult surfaces, such as plastic bags, can be treated with superglue. The glue is heated so that it evaporates (turns into a gas). The vapour sticks to the fingerprints, making them visible. The clearest prints are photographed.

Using a fingerprint scanner is faster and cleaner than inking the fingers and pressing them on a card. The scanned prints can be fed straight into a computer and sent anywhere in the world for checking.

Eliminating prints

Many of the fingerprints found at a crime scene are left by people not involved in the crime. Anyone who visited the crime scene in the days before the crime is fingerprinted. This is done by inking their fingers and pressing them onto a white card, or by using a fingerprint scanner. Each finger is pressed on the scanner, which scans the print and saves it in a computer. Unless there is a reason to suspect any of these people, they are eliminated from the investigation. Any prints that are still unidentified may belong to the person who committed the crime. They will be compared to fingerprints taken from suspects.

Making casts

Some pieces of evidence are too fragile to move, for instance footprints and tyre prints in soft ground. Such evidence is photographed and casts are made. To make a cast, a material called dental stone is poured on the print. It sets hard and makes a permanent copy of the print. If a tool has been used to force a door or window open, a cast may be made of any mark left behind. Quick-setting plastic is pressed against the tool mark. When it is peeled off, it contains a permanent record of the mark.

The body inspectors

If a dead body is found at a crime scene, it is examined by a **forensic** pathologist. Then it is packed into a new body bag and taken to the **morgue**. A new bag is used so that the body is not contaminated with evidence from any other death. The body is moved with great care so that it is not marked or damaged.

Plaster casts of tyre prints at a crime scene can be compared to the tyres on suspect vehicles.

THE SCIENCE YOU LEARN: CATALYSTS

A catalyst is a substance that helps a **chemical reaction** to happen. Luminol works because of a catalyst. Just before luminol is used, it is mixed with hydrogen peroxide. If iron is added to this mixture, it acts as a catalyst and causes a chemical reaction that gives out light. The red colour of blood is produced by a substance called **haemoglobin**, which contains iron. If luminol mixes with blood, the iron in blood triggers the chemical reaction and produces a glow.

CUTTING EDGE: UNDERSTANDING MINDS AND BEHAVIOUR

Psychologists can learn about a criminal's personality and lifestyle by looking at a crime scene. This is called psychological profiling. It can help police narrow down their search for a suspect.

In the United States, the Federal Bureau of Investigation's (FBI's) Behavioural Sciences Unit specializes in the study of criminal behaviour. Their Violent Criminal Apprehension Program (ViCAP) records details of violent crimes and searches for similarities between them. It searches for crimes so similar that they may have been committed by the same person. ViCAP can give an early warning that a serial killer is at work. A similar system called the Violent Crime Linkage Analysis System (ViCLAS) was developed in Canada. Many people find ViCLAS more user-friendly than ViCAP. Other countries, including France, Germany, Ireland, the Netherlands, New Zealand, Switzerland, and the United Kingdom, also now use ViCLAS.

Cleaning up

A crime scene may have been cleaned to hide evidence. If investigators think blood might have been cleaned up, they spray the area with a chemical called **luminol**. They turn the lights out and the luminol glows wherever there was blood.

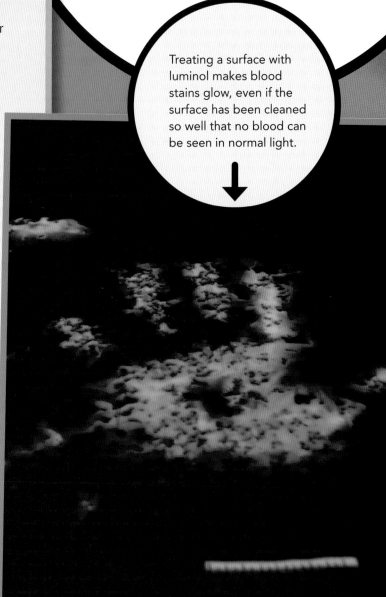

Treating a surface with luminol makes blood stains glow, even if the surface has been cleaned so well that no blood can be seen in normal light.

Analysing the evidence

The evidence from a crime scene is analysed to find out what it means. This work is done by forensic scientists in a crime laboratory. Each piece of evidence arriving at a crime lab must not touch or contaminate any other piece of evidence. The tests carried out must be accurate and reliable, because the future of someone accused of a crime may depend on them.

Labs within labs

A large crime lab is actually a set of smaller labs. Each of them deals with a different branch of forensic science. One might specialize in firearms, while another deals with trace evidence, such as hair and fibres, and another deals with fingerprints, and so on.

Each piece of evidence may be tested several times in different ways by a series of specialists. A knife used in a violent attack might be checked for fingerprints, examined by a trace evidence expert for hairs and fibres, and examined by a blood expert. At each step, a record is made to show who took the evidence out of storage and when, which tests were carried out, and when the evidence was returned to secure storage.

A modern crime laboratory is a busy workplace, with scientists carrying out tests on evidence collected from crime scenes and suspects. This laboratory specializes in blood tests.

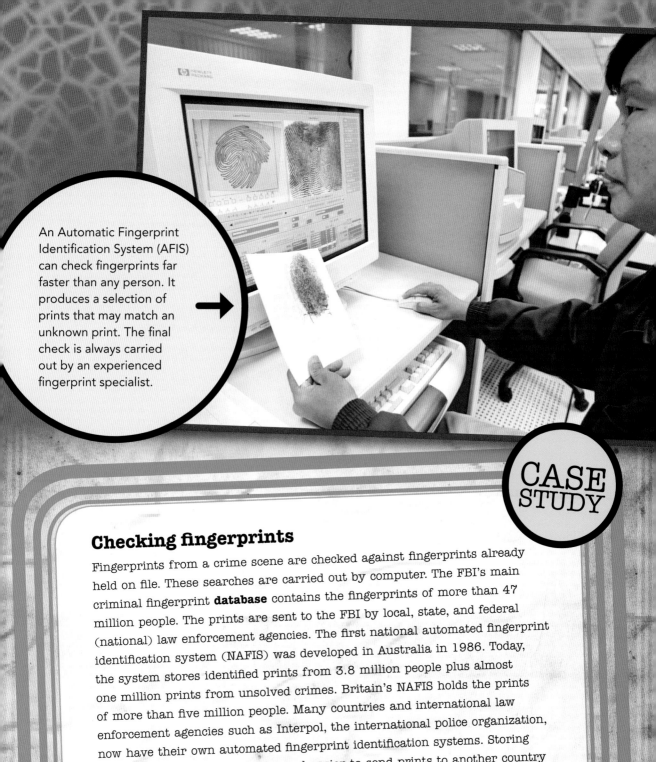

An Automatic Fingerprint Identification System (AFIS) can check fingerprints far faster than any person. It produces a selection of prints that may match an unknown print. The final check is always carried out by an experienced fingerprint specialist.

CASE STUDY

Checking fingerprints

Fingerprints from a crime scene are checked against fingerprints already held on file. These searches are carried out by computer. The FBI's main criminal fingerprint **database** contains the fingerprints of more than 47 million people. The prints are sent to the FBI by local, state, and federal (national) law enforcement agencies. The first national automated fingerprint identification system (NAFIS) was developed in Australia in 1986. Today, the system stores identified prints from 3.8 million people plus almost one million prints from unsolved crimes. Britain's NAFIS holds the prints of more than five million people. Many countries and international law enforcement agencies such as Interpol, the international police organization, now have their own automated fingerprint identification systems. Storing prints digitally makes it faster and easier to send prints to another country to confirm the identity of a suspect being held there.

The shape, thickness, colour, and surface texture of hairs enables forensic scientists to match two or more hairs and say whether or not they come from the same person. →

Hair and fibres

When two people struggle with each other, hair and clothes fibres from one are transferred to the other. Even rubbing against a door or a piece of furniture can leave a few fibres behind. A knife or a blunt weapon often picks up hair or fibres from the victim of an attack.

Human or animal

Experienced investigators can look at a hair under a microscope and tell immediately whether it is human or animal hair. Animal hair has scales on the surface. The pattern of the scales is different for different animal species (types). It is even possible to tell what part of a human body hair came from by looking at the shape of the hair's cross-section. Head hair is round, beard hair is triangular, and armpit hair is oval. If human hair has been bleached or dyed, this can also be seen under a microscope. If the hair has roots, the root cells can be used to produce a **DNA profile** of their owner (see pages 18–19).

IN YOUR HOME: HAIR AND FIBRES

Wipe a surface or brush a carpet in your home and you will find hair, fibres, and dust. Everyone sheds three or four hairs each hour. Pets also shed hair. House-dust is mainly made of dead skin. The fibres are a mixture of natural and synthetic fibres from carpets, clothes, and other fabrics. There may also be particles of sand and soil that have been walked in on people's shoes. The mixture is probably unique to your home.

Finding fibres

In the past, people's clothes were mainly made of natural fibres such as wool, cotton, and linen. These fibres are easy to identify under a microscope. Today, fabrics often contain synthetic fibres such as rayon, nylon, and polyester. Synthetic fibres can look very similar because they are made in a similar way. Liquid plastic is forced through tiny holes to produce the long thin threads, or filaments.

Luckily, there is a way to identify the different types of synthetic fibre. Coloured glass looks coloured because it absorbs (soaks up) some colours of light and lets other colours pass through. In a similar way, synthetic fibres absorb some invisible **infrared** waves and reflect others. Each type of fibre lets a unique selection of waves pass through. The waves that pass through a fibre are analysed to find out what material the fibre is made from. This is called infrared spectrophotometry.

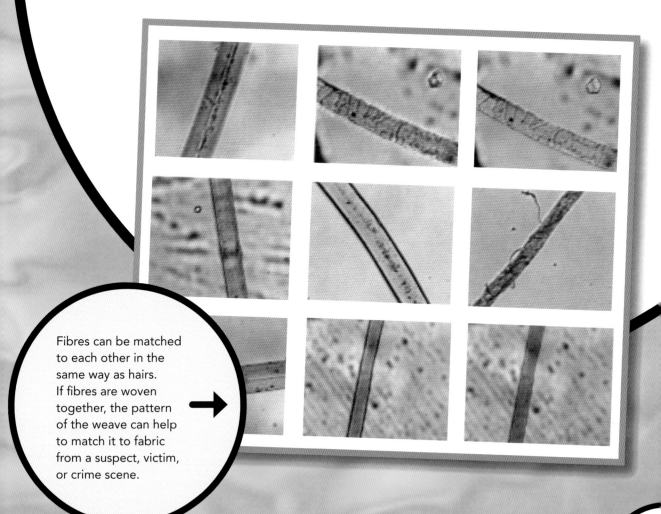

Fibres can be matched to each other in the same way as hairs. If fibres are woven together, the pattern of the weave can help to match it to fabric from a suspect, victim, or crime scene.

Blood

Blood found at a crime scene holds a lot of information. Specialists called forensic **serologists** analyse it biologically. Other experts analyse the size, shape, and patterns of drips and splashes, called **spatter**.

Blood spatter is very revealing. Blood dripping straight downwards produces circular spots. If the spots have spiky edges, called crenellation, the blood fell from higher up than drips without any crenellation. Long, thin splashes show that the blood hit the surface at an angle. Streaks of blood all pointing in the same direction on a wall or ceiling may have sprayed off the end of a bloodstained weapon as it was used.

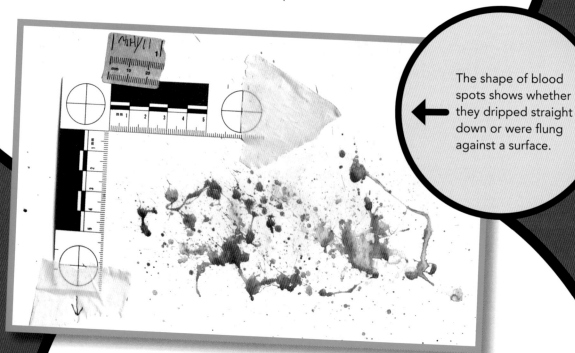

The shape of blood spots shows whether they dripped straight down or were flung against a surface.

Is it really blood?

When investigators find blood, they must confirm that it really is blood. A tiny sample of the stain is mixed with a chemical that changes colour when it reacts with blood. A test that confirms something the investigator already suspects is called a presumptive test.

How old is it?

Blood changes colour as it breaks down. It can be anything from bright red to black. An experienced investigator can judge how old a blood stain is just by looking at it. An instrument called a **spectrophotometer** does the same job by measuring the stain's colour.

THE SCIENCE YOU LEARN: BLOOD GROUPS

Everyone's blood belongs to one of four main blood groups, called A, B, AB, and O. They were discovered by a Viennese doctor, Karl Landsteiner (1868–1943), in 1901. Since then, more substances, called factors, have been found in blood. One of the best-known is called the rhesus factor, because it was discovered in experiments with rhesus monkeys. As well as belonging to one of the four main blood groups, blood is either rhesus positive or rhesus negative. All the factors found so far divide blood into about 288 groups.

Where did it come from?

The next step is to confirm that the blood is human. A little of the blood and some test solution are dripped onto a glass plate or into a test tube. If the blood is human, a cloudy band appears where the blood and test solution meet.

Another test shows which **blood group** the unknown sample belongs to. Blood groups are not like fingerprints. Many people share the same blood group. However, knowing an offender's blood group from a crime scene sample can narrow down the search for the offender.

Sometimes, a forensic scientist can find out someone's blood group even if no blood was left at the crime scene! About 80 percent of people are known as secretors. This means that their body fluids, such as tears, saliva, and semen, contain blood cells. If these body fluids are left at a crime scene, they can be analysed to find the blood group.

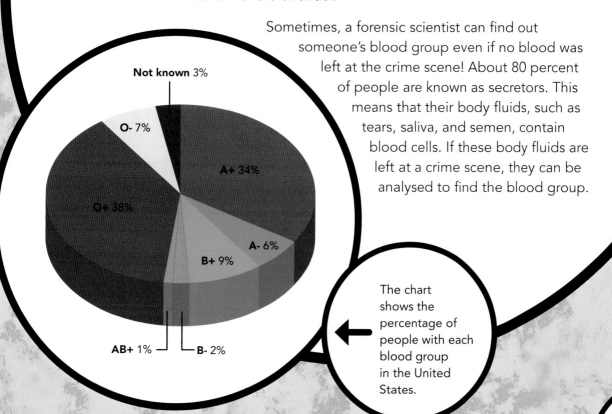

Not known 3%
O- 7%
A+ 34%
O+ 38%
A- 6%
B+ 9%
AB+ 1%
B- 2%

The chart shows the percentage of people with each blood group in the United States.

DNA

Our bodies are made up of billions of cells. Each cell contains the instructions, or genetic code, that created the person. The genetic code is made of a substance called deoxyribonucleic acid (**DNA**). Only identical twins have the same DNA. Everyone else's DNA is different. Forensic scientists can compare DNA found at a crime scene with DNA taken from suspects and victims to see if they match.

Genetic fingerprints

DNA from a crime scene is compared to DNA from a suspect by producing a DNA profile, or genetic fingerprint. DNA profiling was invented in 1984 by Sir Alec Jeffreys at the University of Leicester. It is a way of making the differences between people's genetic code visible and easy to compare. About 99.9 percent of human DNA is the same for everyone. It is just the last 0.1 percent that produces all the differences between people. Some of the genetic code in this DNA repeats itself over and over again. The number of repeats at particular points in the code varies from person to person. DNA profiling compares the number of repeats from different people.

If the letters that form the entire DNA sequence in one human cell were printed, they would fill 200 books, each with 1,000 pages! If the DNA from one cell was unwound and laid in a line, it would be nearly 2 metres (6 feet) long!

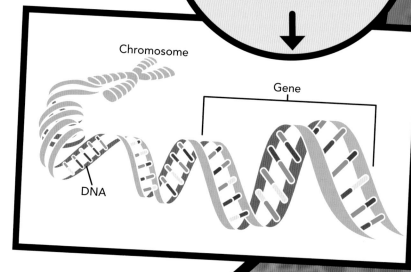

Chromosome

Gene

DNA

 THE SCIENCE YOU LEARN: DNA

DNA is a long molecule in the shape of a twisted ladder. Each rung of the ladder is made of two chemicals called bases. There are only four bases, called adenine, thymine, cytosine, and guanine. It is the order of these bases along the length of the DNA molecule that forms the genetic code. The DNA in a cell's nucleus is divided into units called **chromosomes**. Humans have 23 pairs of chromosomes, 46 in all. The chromosomes are chains of smaller units called **genes**. The genes make substances called proteins, which build the body and make it work.

DNA profiling

First, DNA is extracted from cells. The pieces of DNA needed for a profile are then cut out of the long strands using **enzymes**. The enzymes cut the DNA at particular points. The pieces of DNA are a jumble of different lengths. They are separated by a process called electrophoresis. The DNA is placed at one end of a sheet of gel. Electricity moves the DNA pieces through the gel. Short pieces move faster than long pieces and so they spread out. The pattern of long and short pieces is transferred onto a sheet of film called an autoradiogram to make it easier to see. If the patterns from two different DNA samples match, they probably came from the same person.

Sir Alec Jeffreys, the inventor of DNA profiling, studied biochemistry at Oxford University. He is now a professor of genetics at the University of Leicester.

Documents

Forensic scientists often have to examine documents and decide whether they are genuine. To check handwriting, a document specialist compares samples of handwriting. No matter how good a **forgery** is, the writer cannot copy every shape, line, and angle of someone else's writing.

A genuine note or diary entry may have been altered to change its meaning. Alterations are detected by looking at the writing under ultraviolet, infrared, and laser light. Under these lights, the ink used to make the changes will glow differently from the rest of the writing.

If something was written on the top sheet of a notepad, an imprint of the writing is pressed into the sheets below it. The imprint can be read by lighting the paper from the side or by carrying out an ESDA (Electrostatic Detection Apparatus) test. The sheet of paper to be tested is placed on top of the ESDA machine and covered with a thin plastic sheet. Air is sucked from under the paper. This pulls the plastic sheet against the paper so that it follows the shape of any writing impressions in it. Then the sheet is charged with electricity and black powder is poured onto it. Most of the powder slides off, but the electric charge pulls some of it into the impressions in the paper, making the writing visible.

The ESDA test makes the imprint of writing on a piece of paper clearly visible and easy to read.

Specks

The tiniest specks of evidence can yield vital information. Tiny fragments of glass from a crime scene may be picked up by an offender's clothes. Forensic scientists can match this glass to glass at the crime scene. They measure a property called the refractive index. It shows how much the glass bends light passing through it. Different types of glass have different refractive indexes. Scientists also measure the tiny amounts of different trace elements in the glass. If the refractive index and trace elements of two samples of glass match, they probably came from the same source.

Pollen or seeds caught in someone's clothes can show where they were and when, because plants produce pollen and seeds only at certain times of the year.

CASE STUDY

Soil evidence

When police found an abandoned car near Adelaide, Australia, in September 2000, the only clue to the whereabouts of the owner and her son was a muddy shovel. Soil scientist Dr Rob Fitzpatrick analysed soil on the shovel. It was a sloppy wet mixture of iron oxides and clay, with small fragments of rock typically found at mines and quarries. The acidity and salinity (saltiness) of the soil were also measured. Comparing the test results with a geological map of the area led investigators to a quarry in the Adelaide Hills. Soil from the quarry was tested and it exactly matched the soil on the shovel. Investigators located the wettest part of the quarry and discovered two bodies.

Fire and explosion

Not all fires and explosions happen by accident. Some are caused deliberately. The crime of starting a fire is called arson.

Investigators try to find out where a fire started. Heat, smoke, and flames rise, so investigators start at the lowest point of a burned building. Accidental fires usually start in one place, called the point of origin. If investigators find more than one point of origin, they may suspect arson.

A flammable substance, such as petrol, may have been used to start a fire. A substance like this is called an accelerant because it accelerates (speeds up) the growth and spread of the fire.

THE SCIENCE YOU LEARN: COMBUSTION

Burning, also called **combustion**, is a chemical reaction. It happens when a substance combines with a gas, usually oxygen in the air, in a chemical reaction that gives out light and heat. A chemical reaction can be written down as an equation. The substances on the left combine and form the substances on the right. The arrow between them shows the direction of the reaction. The equation for burning methane (natural gas) is:

$$CH_4 + 2O_2 \rightarrow CO_2 + 2H_2O + energy$$

Methane Oxygen Carbon dioxide Water vapour heat/light

Fire investigators are trained to look for the signs of arson in the jumble of burned wood and twisted metal left behind after a fire.

Investigators use electronic noses called vapour sniffers to test for accelerants in the air. Small pieces of material can also be tested for accelerants.

Explosives

There are two main types of explosive: low explosives and high explosives. Low explosives include gunpowder and flammable gas. When a low explosive is set on fire, it just burns – unless it is enclosed in a container. Then the container bursts, causing an explosion.

When a flammable gas catches fire, the heat of the flame makes the gas expand. As it expands, it becomes less dense than the surrounding air and floats upwards.

THE SCIENCE YOU LEARN: EXPLOSION

An explosion is a sudden outburst of energy caused when a chemical reaction gives out a lot of energy and produces huge volumes of gas very quickly. For example, when only 10 ml (0.3 oz) of a powerful explosive called nitroglycerine explodes, it expands 10,000 times almost instantly, producing 100 litres (22 gallons) of gas. The chemical equation for this reaction is:

$$4(C_3H_5N_3O_9) \rightarrow 12\ CO_2 + 10\ H_2O + 6N_2 + O_2$$

Nitroglycerine → Carbon dioxide + Water vapour + Nitrogen + Oxygen

The pressure soars and the gas flies out in all directions. The gas flies outwards at nearly 11,000 kph (7,000 mph), which is nearly 100 times faster than a hurricane-force wind!

High explosives

Burning does not set off a high explosive. Instead, a small explosion from a detonator is usually needed. High explosives are more powerful than low explosives. When a bomb goes off, the explosive and its container are shattered into tiny fragments and flung in all directions.

When a bomb has exploded inside a car, the car's body peels open like a burst balloon. When investigators see this type of damage, they immediately suspect a crime.

Air crash investigation

After an air crash, investigators must find out whether a plane crashed because of pilot error, mechanical failure, or crime. One of the first questions they ask is – did the plane fall from the sky in one piece or did it break up in mid-air? If a plane crashes in one piece, all the wreckage is concentrated in one small area. If it breaks up in mid-air, the wreckage falls over a much bigger area. If the plane broke up in mid-air, the next question is – did it suffer structural failure or did a bomb explode inside it?

Air crash investigators search for the plane's two black boxes. The flight data recorder records information about the plane, including its speed, height, tilt, engine data, and control positions. The cockpit voice recorder records the pilots' voices and other sounds on the flight deck. These two "black boxes" are actually orange, to make them easier to find. They can survive a crash, fire, and water. Analysing the data in the black boxes may reveal what happened to the plane.

An airliner's black box can give investigators vital clues to what happened to an aircraft just before a crash.

Pan Am 103

On 21 December 1988, Pan Am flight 103 took off from Heathrow Airport, bound for New York, USA. As the plane flew over the Scottish town of Lockerbie, it exploded. The wreckage fell over a huge area. All 259 people on the plane and 11 people on the ground died.

Investigators examined 180,000 pieces of evidence. They found tiny, fingernail-sized pieces of circuit board that came from an electronic timer and a radio cassette player. These discoveries and chemical tests revealed that the plane had been blown up by a bomb made from an explosive called Semtex. It had been packed inside a radio cassette player in a suitcase. A small fragment of shirt found with the pieces of circuit board was traced to a clothing company in Malta. Trousers found near the shirt were also traced to a shop in Malta. The shop's owner helped produce an artist's impression of the man who had bought them. Then the timer was identified and the manufacturer in Switzerland gave investigators information that led them to Libya and, finally, the identification of the person responsible for the bombing.

Autopsy

An **autopsy** is a surgical operation carried out to find out why a person died. First, the body is carefully examined. Marks and injuries are noted and photographed. Then the body is opened. The brain and organs are taken out, examined, and weighed. The contents of the stomach and intestines are examined. Samples are taken to be studied further.

If the body was found in a burning building, the airway from the mouth and nose to the lungs is examined. An airway blackened by smoke shows that the victim was breathing when the fire started. No blackening means that the victim was already dead when the fire started. If the body was found in water, water inside and outside the body are compared. The two should be identical. If they don't match, the person may not have died where the body was found.

THE SCIENCE YOU LEARN: BODY TEMPERATURE

The body temperature of a healthy adult is about 36.8°C (98.6°F). The heat is produced by chemical reactions that break down food and make muscles work. These chemical reactions stop at the time of death and the body starts cooling down. It cools down by about 0.8°C (1.5°F) an hour.

An autopsy is carried out by a specially trained physician called a Medical Examiner or forensic pathologist to try to find out how someone died.

CUTTING EDGE: THE BODY FARM

If a body is badly decayed, the usual methods for working out the time of death do not work. However, the state of decay itself is a clue. Scientists at the Body Farm at the University of Tennessee in the United States, research human body decay. Human bodies are left in the open to decay, while students study them. The Body Farm can recreate any situation that occurs in a real investigation. Some of the bodies are laid on the ground. Others are buried or left in cars.

Time of death

Several methods are used to find out the time of death:

- After death, the body cools down. The body temperature taken at the crime scene gives an idea of the time interval since death.
- Chemical changes make the muscles stiffen. This is called rigor mortis. It starts around 3 hours after death, spreads through the body over 12–18 hours, and starts to disappear in another 18 hours.
- Blood sinks to the lowest part of the body and stains the skin in about six hours.
- After about two days, bacteria growing on the skin turn it a green colour.
- Flies and other insects lay eggs on a body. The stage of their life cycle gives another clue to how long the body has been lying.
- Hair and nails do not continue growing after death so do not help indicate time of death.

The temperature of a body falls steadily after death until it reaches the same temperature as its surroundings.

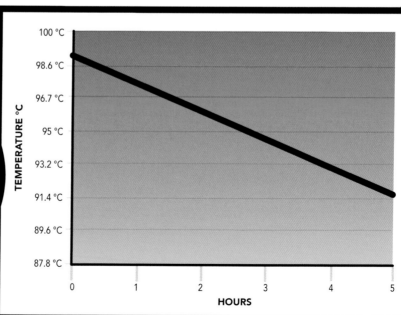

INVESTIGATION:
IDENTIFYING MYSTERY SUBSTANCES

Samples of unknown substances from an autopsy or crime scene are identified by a piece of equipment called a gas chromatograph **mass spectrometer** (GC-MS). The same equipment is also used to test samples of body fluids from living people for drugs and poisons.

A GC-MS is really two instruments in one – a gas chromatograph and a mass spectrometer. A scientist injects a small sample of the unknown substance into the gas chromatograph. The substance is heated to change it to a gas.

The sample travels through a long, thin tube called a column. An **inert** gas, such as helium, flows through the column and carries the sample with it. The column is filled with a fine sand-like powder. The various molecules in the unknown substance travel through the tiny spaces between the particles in the column. Small molecules travel through the column faster than big molecules. Therefore the smallest molecules come out of the end of the column first, followed by bigger molecules.

Which molecule is which?

The different molecules in the sample have been separated from each other, but now they must be identified. The time they take to come out of the column gives a strong clue to what they are, but similar molecules take similar times to go through the column. To identify them beyond doubt, they are analysed by the mass spectrometer.

The molecules coming out of the column are bombarded with **electrons**. This breaks them up and gives them an electric charge. Then they fly through a **magnetic field**. The magnetism bends their straight flight-path into a curve.

The tightness of the curve depends on the mass of the molecule. Small, light molecules make a tighter turn than bigger, heavier molecules. Changing the strength of the magnetic field alters the shape of the curve too. The machine adjusts the strength of the magnetic field to make each type of molecule hit a detector. The strength of the magnetic field needed to make each type of molecule hit the detector shows how heavy the molecule is. The size of the electric charge on the molecules shows how many there are.

The types and amounts of the different molecules appear as a series of spikes on a computer screen. Each spike represents a different molecule. The height of the spike shows how much of it there is. Using this information, a scientist can tell what the unknown substance is.

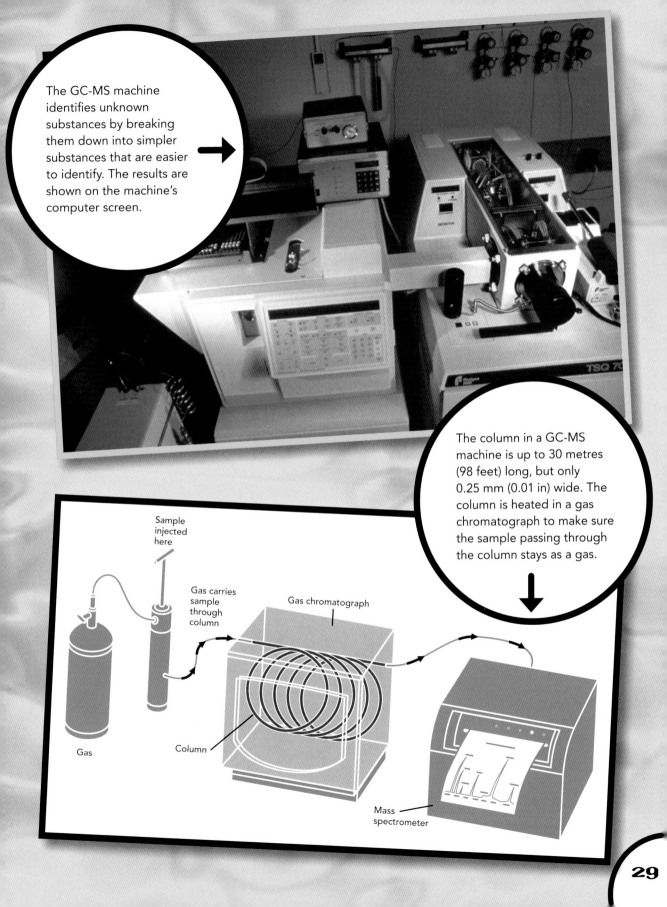

The GC-MS machine identifies unknown substances by breaking them down into simpler substances that are easier to identify. The results are shown on the machine's computer screen.

The column in a GC-MS machine is up to 30 metres (98 feet) long, but only 0.25 mm (0.01 in) wide. The column is heated in a gas chromatograph to make sure the sample passing through the column stays as a gas.

Sample injected here

Gas carries sample through column

Gas chromatograph

Gas

Column

Mass spectrometer

INVESTIGATION: PAPER CHROMATOGRAPHY

Liquid **chromatography** separates a liquid into the substances that it contains. The liquid moves through a layer of gel on a glass plate. Smaller molecules in the liquid move faster than big molecules. The molecules get spread out across the plate.

You can see how it works by doing a simple experiment. Use a felt-tip pen to put a big dot of ink about 3 cm (1.2 in) up from the bottom of a strip of filter paper or blotting paper. Put 1 cm (0.4 in) of water in the bottom of a glass. Hang the strip of paper from a pencil sitting across the top of the glass. The paper must dip into the water. The ink must be above the water. Water rises up the paper and carries the ink with it. The small molecules move faster than the big molecules. The ink separates out into the different colours that it contains.

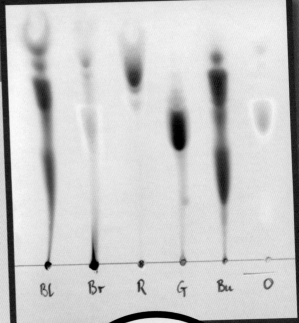

Ink contains different colours mixed together. Investigators can use chromatography to compare two ink samples.

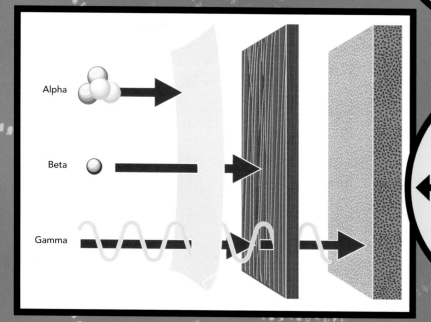

Alpha

Beta

Gamma

Alpha particles are easily stopped by paper. Beta particles go through paper, but are stopped by a thin sheet of wood. Gamma rays are stopped only by a thick concrete block or lead sheet.

Radiation

There are a few rare cases of people being killed by consuming a radioactive substance. If someone has died as a result of **radiation**, it is dangerous to perform an autopsy on the body.

Radiation crime

In 2006, Russian ex-spy Alexander Litvinenko fell ill and died in London. The cause of his illness was a mystery. It was eventually found that he had been killed by radiation. Radiation can break up molecules inside living cells. The most important molecule in a cell is DNA. If DNA is damaged by radiation, it may not work normally. One type of radiation damage makes a cell divide and multiply uncontrollably, causing cancer. A higher dose of radiation may cause so much damage that a cell dies. If lots of cells die, whole organs may fail and cause death.

Most radioactive substances give out **gamma rays**, which are easily detected outside the body. Litvinenko had been given a rare substance called Polonium-210, which mainly gives out **alpha radiation**. Inside the body, these radiation particles are stopped by the organs and tissues around them. The radiation can not be detected outside the body. The cause of Litvinenko's illness was discovered when his blood and urine were found to be radioactive.

Alexander Litvinenko was killed by a lethal dose of radiation from a very rare substance called Polonium-210.

🧠 THE SCIENCE YOU LEARN: RADIATION

Radiation is the name for the particles and energy given out by atoms. The most intense radiation is known as ionizing radiation, because it can change atoms into electrically charged particles called ions. There are three types of ionizing radiation, called alpha, **beta**, and gamma. Alpha and beta radiation are made of particles. Gamma radiation is made of electromagnetic waves, which are like light waves, but shorter and more intense.

Identification

Investigators often have to identify people who will not, or cannot, identify themselves. The person responsible for a crime may have been seen, but their identity could remain unknown. A suspect in **custody** (prison) may give a false identity, or none at all. A discovered body may carry no means of identification.

When a crime is committed, witnesses may have seen someone behaving oddly, or running away. A forensic artist can turn their descriptions into a lifelike sketch. Some computer systems can do the same thing. They build up a face from a database of hair, eyes, noses, mouths, and other features. The sketch or computer image is then shown to people in the hope that someone will recognize and identify the face.

Body of evidence

The identification of a body is usually straightforward. A friend or family member can look at the body and confirm the identity. Fingerprints and unique marks, such as tattoos and scars, might be used as an extra check. However, if a body is too badly damaged or decomposed to be identified in these ways, other methods are used. The body's DNA can be compared to the DNA of possible relatives. An identical twin of the unknown person would have the same DNA. A parent or child would share half of their DNA with the unknown person.

Photo ID

If the identity of a decomposed body is suspected, family photographs can help to confirm the identity. A photograph of a skull and a photograph of the person in life are enlarged to the same size. One photo is laid on top of the other. If the skull belongs to the person in the photo, the skull and photo should match exactly in every way. The positions and sizes of all the facial features should be identical. A photo showing the person smiling is especially useful, because the teeth in the photo can be compared to the teeth in the skull.

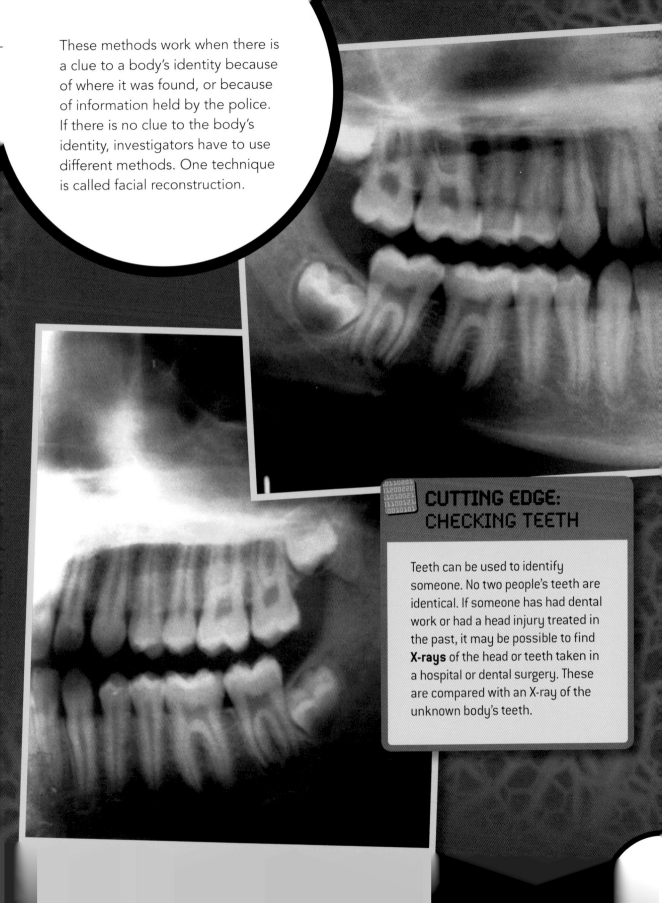

These methods work when there is a clue to a body's identity because of where it was found, or because of information held by the police. If there is no clue to the body's identity, investigators have to use different methods. One technique is called facial reconstruction.

CUTTING EDGE: CHECKING TEETH

Teeth can be used to identify someone. No two people's teeth are identical. If someone has had dental work or had a head injury treated in the past, it may be possible to find **X-rays** of the head or teeth taken in a hospital or dental surgery. These are compared with an X-ray of the unknown body's teeth.

Facial reconstruction

In forensic science, facial reconstruction means recreating how a person may have looked from their skull. It involves a lot more than just wrapping the skull with artificial skin. The shape of the face depends on the shape of the skull plus all the muscles and other tissues beneath the skin.

A reconstruction artist starts with a model of the skull. The depth of tissue at dozens of points on the skull is marked by sticking pegs to the bone. Each peg is the same length as the depth of the tissue at each point. Then muscles made of clay are added to the skull. More clay is added to model the rest of the soft tissue. The clay is built up to the right thickness, using the pegs as a guide.

So far, this process is based on science. However, to make the head look lifelike, it needs hair and a facial expression. The artist has to guess the hair colour, length, and style, and also the facial expression. Even with this guesswork, facial reconstruction can produce very lifelike results. The clay head doesn't have to be identical to the person's appearance in life. If it is close enough to jog someone's memory and lead to the identification of the person, then it has done its job.

Facial reconstruction in clay requires a combination of art and science. The people who do it have to understand the anatomy of the facial bones and muscles. They also need the practical skill and artistic talent of a sculptor.

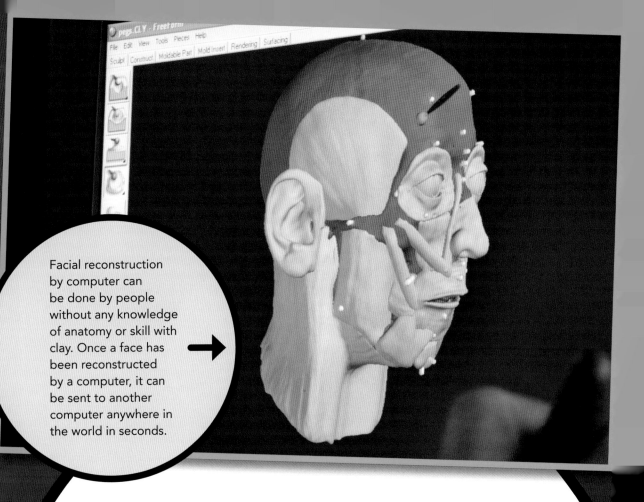

Facial reconstruction by computer can be done by people without any knowledge of anatomy or skill with clay. Once a face has been reconstructed by a computer, it can be sent to another computer anywhere in the world in seconds.

Computer reconstruction

Computer reconstruction can be done without clay or any other modelling material. The skull is scanned by a laser. This sends the precise shape of the skull to a computer. The computer adds muscle and tissue to the right depth and lays a life-like skin on top. The realistic look of the face is achieved using photographs of living people. If forensic scientists can tell that the unidentified body belongs to a white woman in her 20s, for example, lots of photographs of white women in their 20s are combined by the computer to produce a typical face. Then this face is draped over the computer-generated head to produce an image that should be similar to the unidentified person in life.

Stone Age faces

The technique of facial reconstruction was pioneered in Russia in the 1920s. Russian anthropologist Mikhail Gerasimov (1907–1970) measured the tissue depth on the faces of bodies that were used for teaching medical students. He used this information to recreate the faces of Stone Age people, using fossil skulls. In 1939, his reconstruction of a modern skull helped to solve a murder.

A forensic anthropologist tries to solve the mystery of a discovered skeleton by reading the clues in the bones. →

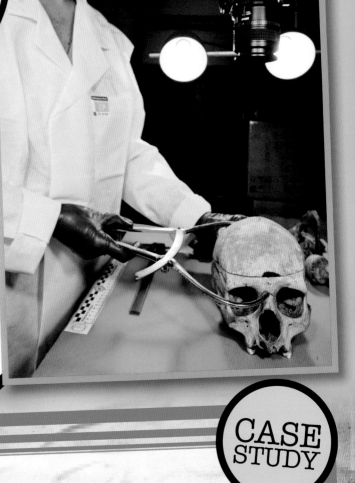

Reading skeletons

Anthropology is the study of humankind. A physical anthropologist specializes in the study of human remains. Forensic anthropologists use their expertise in physical anthropology to help crime investigators find out about discovered human remains.

By looking at a skeleton, a forensic anthropologist can tell the sex, height, age, and ethnic origin of the person.

CASE STUDY

Key evidence

When boys fishing in the Ohio River in Connecticut, USA, found a skeleton, forensic anthropologist Dr Emily Craig was called. She was able to tell police that the skeleton belonged to a man 193 cm (6 ft 4 in) tall, weighing at least 113 kg (250 pounds), and that he had been shot in the head. A search of his clothing produced a set of keys made in Connecticut and a money clip with a pair of initials on it. This enabled police to identify the man as someone who had disappeared 34 years earlier.

CUTTING EDGE: WORKING WITH BONE FRAGMENTS

Sometimes, a forensic anthropologist does not have a whole skeleton to work with. When Professor Sue Black was called to examine partly-burned human remains discovered in Wolverhampton in the West Midlands, she found 2,500 fragments of bone, each no bigger than a fingernail! Even so, she was able to tell police that the bones belonged to a woman less than 150 cm (5 ft) tall, and between 17 and 19 years of age. Searching through missing persons records enabled the police to identify her.

How old?

A forensic anthropologist can tell a body's age age from the skeleton in several ways:

- When a baby is born, there are gaps between the bones of the skull. These close up by the age of 15 months, but they can still be seen in X-rays until 2 years of age.
- Up to the age of 15, the teeth grow in a well-known order.
- While someone is growing, the ends of their bones are soft. They harden as the person grows older. There are about 800 of these points in a skeleton and they harden at different rates up to about the age of 25.
- Older people suffer from conditions that affect the bones, such as arthritis and osteoporosis. These and other conditions give important clues to age.

Sex and height

The shape of the skull and hip bones shows whether a skeleton belongs to a man or a woman. A man's skull has lumps of bone called brow ridges above the eyes. A woman's skull has no brow ridges. The parts of the skull that muscles are attached to are bigger in men. Men also have narrower hips than women.

Measuring the skeleton and adding about 10 cm (4 in) for the missing muscles and soft tissue gives the person's height. If some bones are missing, the height can be calculated from the length of long bones such as the femur (thigh bone). A person's height is roughly two and two-thirds the length of the femur.

Firearms

The branch of science that deals with guns and bullets is called ballistics. Firing a gun releases a wealth of evidence linking the shooter, the gun, and the bullet.

When a gun is fired, a part called the hammer hits the end of a cartridge and sets off a tiny explosive pellet called the **primer**. This sets off the main charge, called the **propellant**. The propellant burns and produces a lot of gas very quickly. The gas pressure forces the bullet out of the cartridge case and pushes it down the gun barrel. The bullet is a tight fit inside the barrel so that the gas doesn't leak out around the bullet.

Grooves spiral around the inside of the barrel and make the bullet spin. The grooves are called **rifling**. The metal of the barrel is a lot harder than the soft lead bullet, so the rifling carves marks in the bullet. These marks are called striations. All the bullets fired by the same gun have the same tell-tale striations. Therefore, a firearms expert can tell which gun fired a particular bullet.

 THE SCIENCE YOU LEARN: PRESSURE

Pressure is the amount of force that presses on a certain area. Increasing the force causes an increase in the pressure. Decreasing the area also causes an increase in the pressure. You can see this in action every time you put something on a notice board. If you press your thumb on the board, it doesn't go through the board. Pressing a drawing pin on the board pushes the pin into the board. The only difference is the area the force is acting on. The point of the pin has a tiny area. All the force from the whole thumb is concentrated at the tip of the pin, producing a lot more pressure than the thumb alone.

Spinning bullets

Bullets are made to spin because a spinning bullet flies further and stays more accurately on target. It works for the same reason that a toy gyroscope keeps spinning in the same direction. The bullet behaves like a flying gyroscope. A bullet that doesn't spin soon starts to tumble as it flies through the air. As it tumbles, the bullet stirs up the air and causes more air resistance. Air resistance acts like a brake and slows the bullet down. The tumbling bullet strays off course and falls to the ground much sooner than a spinning bullet.

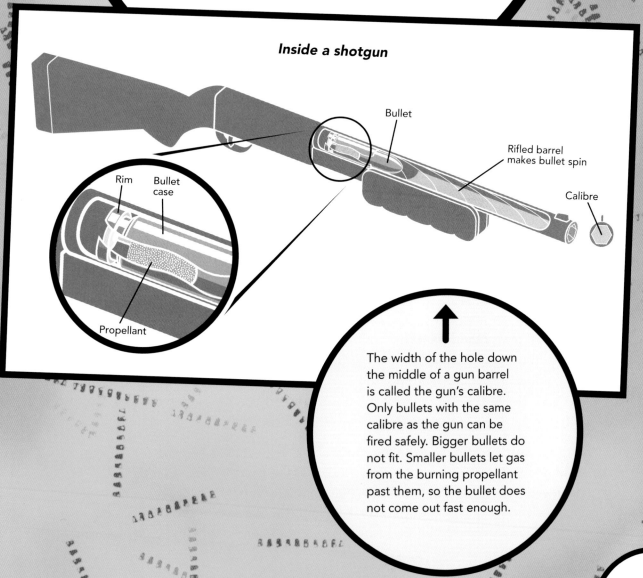

Inside a shotgun

Bullet

Rifled barrel makes bullet spin

Calibre

Rim

Bullet case

Propellant

The width of the hole down the middle of a gun barrel is called the gun's calibre. Only bullets with the same calibre as the gun can be fired safely. Bigger bullets do not fit. Smaller bullets let gas from the burning propellant past them, so the bullet does not come out fast enough.

Comparing bullets

Forensic scientists use a **comparison microscope** to look at two bullets at the same time. One bullet may have been collected from the crime scene. The second bullet may be inside a suspect's gun. Scientists test the second bullet by firing it in a way that won't damage it, such as into a water tank. If the marks on the two bullets line up together, they must have been fired by the same gun.

Cartridge cases

Bullets are made of lead and they are easily damaged when they hit something. Sometimes bullets are too badly damaged to be of any use in tests, but cartridge cases can be just as valuable. The cartridge case is the part that stays in the gun when a bullet is fired. A semi-automatic pistol ejects the cartridge case after firing a bullet. The gun's firing mechanism and ejector mechanism leave scratches and dents on the cartridge case that are unique to each gun.

A shotgun cartridge contains tiny metal balls called lead shot. Lead shot cannot be matched to one particular gun, but the cartridge case can.

Gunshot residue

When someone fires a gun, tiny particles are blown out of the barrel behind the bullet. This is called gunshot residue. The particles travel up to 2 m (6.5 ft) from the gun. The further they go, the more they spread out. Measuring the size of a patch of gunshot residue on a shooting victim shows how close the shooter was.

Gunshot residue also lands on the shooter. If a suspect tests positive for gunshot residue, this can be used in court as proof that the person has fired a gun. However, recent research has shown that people who have never fired a gun can test positive for gunshot residue! Shaking hands with someone who has fired a gun, or walking through an area where a gun has been fired recently, can transfer gunshot residue onto an innocent person.

A forensic scientist uses a microscope to examine a cartridge case collected from a crime scene. Marks on the case enable the scientist to identify the gun it came from.

Trajectories

If bullets have passed through something, investigators can push rods into the holes to show each bullet's flight-path, or trajectory. Tracing bullet trajectories shows the angle and direction of the shots, and whether there was one shooting position or more than one.

Accident or murder?

Sometimes people accused of a gun crime claim that their gun went off by accident. Forensic scientists test this by measuring how much force is needed to pull the gun's trigger. They use an instrument called a trigger pull gauge. If the trigger pull is a lot weaker than it should be, the gun could indeed have been fired by accident. However, if the test shows that the trigger pull is normal, then it is very unlikely that the gun could have gone off accidentally.

Fakes

Paintings and sculptures by famous artists are very valuable. Art forgers try to make fake artworks that look as though they were produced by famous artists, so that they can be sold for huge sums of money. Art experts examine the style, composition, subject, and brush strokes of a painting to make sure they match everything known about the artist. Even if an art forger is good enough to trick the experts, it is more difficult to trick forensic scientists.

An X-ray picture of a painting sometimes reveals another painting underneath it. Canvases were expensive, so they were re-used by painting over older paintings. Paintings were often changed during painting. For example, a background or a figure may have been painted over and repainted in a different position. X-rays reveal these changes too.

Probing paint

Forgers are very good at producing paintings that look old, but scientists can tell whether they just look old or really are old. A genuine old oil painting has microscopic cracks that go all the way through the varnish and paint. A fake old painting may look cracked in the right way, but the cracks are just on the surface. X-rays can probe the surface of the painting and check how far down the cracks go.

Techniques like this are called non-invasive, because they do not damage the painting. If they do not produce the desired results, a small piece of the painting may have to be taken for chemical analysis. It is taken from a part that is normally hidden under the frame.

A chemical analysis of the paint should reveal colours and chemicals that are right for the age of the painting. A blue colour called Prussian blue was not used until 1704, so a painting that is supposed to date from before 1704 should not contain any Prussian blue. Another colour called titanium white was not used until the 1920s, so it should not be found in paintings older than the 1920s.

Testing metal

Works of art made from metal are tested with X-rays. When the rays hit a metal surface, the way they bounce back depends on the surface arrangement of atoms and molecules. The pattern should be the same as for other objects of the same age made of the same metal.

Forgers have been known to make fake sculptures from the ancient world by sticking worthless broken fragments of genuine ancient objects together. Looking inside suspicious statuettes with X-rays reveals how they were assembled, sometimes showing a modern metal frame inside!

CUTTING EDGE: COUNTING RINGS

Oil paintings are painted on canvas stretched over a wooden frame. It may be possible to date the canvas frame using a technique called dendrochronology. It works by matching the tree growth rings in the canvas frame to a database of tree growth rings. If a match is found, it can show when the tree was still growing.

Dating photographs

Photographs made by famous photographers sell for very high prices at auctions. Fraudsters produce modern photographic prints that look old and try to sell them for far more than they are worth. A forensic photograph specialist finds out the age of a photograph by analysing the fibres in the paper and the chemical coatings on the paper. Whitening chemicals called optical brightening agents (OBAs) were added to photographic printing paper in the 1950s. A photograph that is supposed to have been made before this should not have any OBAs in its chemical coating.

THE SCIENCE YOU LEARN: X-RAYS

X-rays are energy waves like light and radio waves, but X-rays are much shorter. Waves such as light, radio, and X-rays are called electromagnetic waves. The shorter the waves, the more energy they have. X-rays have a lot of energy. They can actually pass through some materials. This is how X-ray images are made in hospitals. The rays go through skin and soft tissue more easily than denser substances like bone. In the same way, X-ray pictures of artworks may show something inside them that shouldn't be there and reveal them to be forgeries.

lead case

electron beam

fake statue

X-ray shows metal frame

tungsten anode

X-ray beam

motor

X-rays are produced by firing a beam of electrons at a very hard material such as tungsten metal. When the fast-moving electrons hit the tungsten, they stop in an instant and give out their energy as X-rays.

The Hitler diaries

In 1979, the German magazine *Stern* learned that diaries written by Adolf Hitler (1889–1945), the leader of Nazi Germany during World War II, had been found. Their discovery made headlines all over the world. At first, the diaries seemed to be genuine. However, tests on the paper found chemicals that were not used in papermaking until 1954, nearly 10 years after Hitler's death. Threads attached to the diaries contained polyester and viscose fibres, which were not available when the diaries were supposed to have been made. Four different types of ink were used to write the diaries, but chemical analysis showed that none of them was available in Hitler's time. Ink analysis also showed that the diaries had been written less than a year earlier. All the scientific evidence proved that the diaries were fakes.

↑ Konrad Kujau (left) was the German forger who faked Hitler's diaries. He is seen here presenting them to a German court in Hamburg in 1984.

Conclusion

Forensic scientists are continually trying to stay one step ahead of criminals. When criminals learn how scientists are catching them, they change their behaviour to avoid detection. The competition between scientists and criminals is certain to continue.

The general public know about forensic science and crime investigation thanks to popular television programmes. However, the programmes give the impression that forensic scientists just need an hour or two to solve a crime. It has been called the **CSI** Effect, after a popular television series. Sadly, real life is not like television. Tests that take a few minutes on television can take weeks or months to produce results in reality.

Television scientists sometimes do things that are impossible in the real world. They enlarge a tiny part of a fuzzy security camera picture and enhance it until a sharp image of a car number plate appears. A blurred picture is blurred because a lot of the information needed for a sharp image is missing. It can be cleaned up a bit, but the missing information can not be put back.

Television dramas have shown viewers the work that real forensic scientists do. However, they have also led people to believe, wrongly, that forensic science can reveal every detail of a crime.

Computer power

The amount of information generated by a crime investigation has soared in recent years. It would be impossible to keep track of it all without computers. Computers search through vast amounts of information, which enables investigators to find links between crimes and matches between evidence and people that would have gone unnoticed in the past. As computers become faster and more powerful, they are certain to be even more useful to investigators in the future.

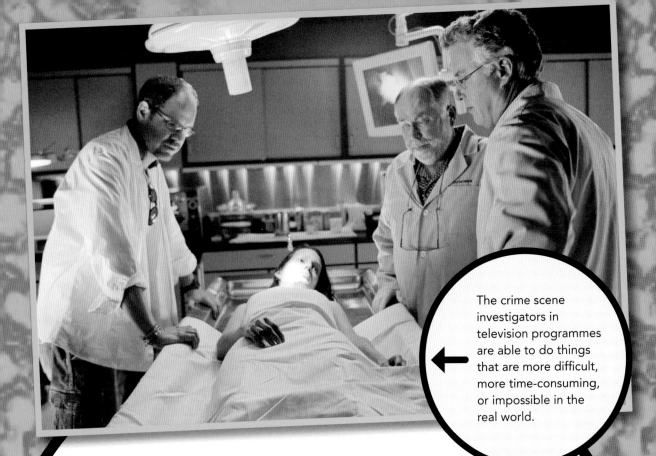

The crime scene investigators in television programmes are able to do things that are more difficult, more time-consuming, or impossible in the real world.

Good or bad? You decide

DNA profiling has become so important in crime-fighting that some countries are setting up DNA databases. When someone is arrested, his or her DNA is taken and compared to the database to see if it matches DNA collected at the scene of a previous crime. The United States and the UK have the world's biggest DNA databases. The United States' database holds DNA from 5 million people. The UK is close behind, with 4.5 million people. Worldwide, the DNA of around 12 million people is stored in databases.

DNA databases would be even more effective in solving crimes if they contained everyone's DNA. Some people think that everybody's DNA profile should be taken at birth. They argue that innocent people have nothing to fear. However, many others believe that governments have no right to collect this information from people who have done nothing wrong. They also worry about how a government or police force might use it in the future, and whether it can really be kept secure and safe from tampering.

Issues like this are not for scientists to decide on. They are issues for people and their governments to resolve.

Facts and figures

Forensic science timeline

1248 A Chinese book called *His Duan Yu* (The Washing Away of Wrongs) explains how to tell the difference between natural deaths and killings. It is the first forensic science book.

1658 British physician Sir Thomas Browne (1605–1682) discovers adipocere, a waxy substance produced by corpses decaying in wet, airless places.

1660 Italian scientist Marcello Malpighi (1628–1694) describes the patterns of ridges on fingertips.

1823 Czech scientist Johan Purkinje (1787–1869) describes different types of fingerprint patterns, including whorls, ellipses, and triangles.

1829 Sir Robert Christison (1797–1882), a professor of forensic medicine in Edinburgh writes a book called *Treatise on Poisons*, which is used for many years by physicians and forensic scientists.

1835 In England, Henry Goddard (1800–1883) is the first person to use bullet comparison to catch a murderer.

1839 Dr John Davey carries out experiments to estimate the time of death by measuring body temperature.

1854 Photography is first used for criminal identification.

1858 British government official William Herschel (1833–1918) begins experimenting with fingerprints in India.

1862 Dutch scientist J Isaak Van Deen (1804–1869) develops a test for blood.

1863 German scientist Christian Frederick Schönbein (1799–1868) discovers that hydrogen peroxide makes haemoglobin foam, leading to a presumptive test for blood.

1880 Henry Faulds (1843–1930), a Scottish missionary working in Japan, is the first person to suggest using fingerprints as a way of identifying criminals.

1883 In Paris, French scientist Alphonse Bertillon (1853–1914) identifies a criminal using the system of measurements he invented. A series of measurements were made of a criminal's head and body. Then when someone is arrested, his measurements are compared to measurements on file to confirm his identity.

1888 Chicago becomes the first city in the United States to use the Bertillon system of identification.

1889 French scientist, Alexandre Lacassagne (1844–1921) shows that a bullet can be matched to the gun that fired it by examining marks made on the bullet by the gun.

1892 In Argentina, fingerprint evidence is used for the first time to convict a murderer.

1892 British scientist Sir Francis Galton (1822–1911) writes a book called *Fingerprints*, which shows the value of fingerprints for identifying people. He divides fingerprints into different patterns called arches, loops, and whorls.

1893 Edward Henry (1850–1931), the British chief of police in Bengal, India, begins using thumb prints as well as the Bertillon system for identifying criminals.

1897 Edward Henry's Indian assistant Azizul Haque invents a way of classifying fingerprints so that they can be used for identification without Bertillon's measurements.

1901 The fingerprint system developed by Azizul Haque is used by British police, although it becomes known as the Henry system.

1901 Austrian scientist Karl Landsteiner (1868–1943) discovers human blood groups.

1904 The United States Bureau of Identification sets up a fingerprint collection.

1910 Edmund Locard (1877–1966), French professor of forensic medicine at the University of Lyon, France, sets up the first police crime laboratory in Lyon.

1920 The comparison microscope is developed by Calvin Goddard, Charles Waite, Phillip Gravelle, and John Fisher.

1924 The first United States police crime laboratory is set up by the Los Angeles Police Department.

1935 Dr Alexander Mearns at the University of Glasgow uses the age of maggots on a body to estimate the time of death of the victim in a murder case.

1967 The United States Federal Bureau of Investigation (FBI) opens the first national law enforcement computing centre, the National Crime Information Center (NCIC).

1975 The Royal Canadian Mounted Police starts using the first automatic fingerprint identification system (AFIS).

1984 British scientist Alec Jeffreys develops DNA profiling.

1986 DNA profiling is used for the first time to catch a murderer.

1992 The FBI sets up a database of the markings on bullets and cartridge cases that can be searched by computer to show links between crimes where the same guns were used.

Forensic science and famous crimes

Research the following famous murder cases and find out how forensic science was used to catch or identify the criminals responsible.

- **The Lindbergh baby kidnapping – USA, 1932**
  Handwriting analysis was vital in the investigation.

- **The murder of Georgi Markov – UK, 1978**
  The extraordinary case of a murder carried out by poison fired from an umbrella!

- **The Alton Coleman case – USA, 1985**
  The use of insect evidence helped to convict this vicious killer.

- **The bombing of Pan Am Flight 103 – UK, 1986**
  Tiny fragments of trace evidence led investigators to the bomber.

- **The Colin Pitchfork case – UK, 1988**
  The first case where DNA profiling was used to catch a murderer.

- **The trial of OJ Simpson – USA, 1995**
  The way the crime scene was managed and the way DNA evidence was collected and stored formed important parts of the defence case.

- **The disappearance of Peter Falconio – Australia, 2001**
  DNA evidence trapped an attacker in a controversial case.

- **The murder of Alexander Litvinenko – UK, 2006**
  Forensic science was able to prove that a rare radioactive substance was used to commit murder.

Famous forensic scientists

- **William Bass**
  Bass set up The Body Farm at the University of Tennessee in the United States in 1981, to study the stages of human decomposition after death.

- **Sir Alec Jeffreys**
  The British geneticist who invented DNA profiling in 1984.

- **Thomas Noguchi**

  Retired American chief medical examiner-coroner and professor of forensic pathology. Known as the "coroner to the stars" because of the amount of autopsies he performed on famous people.

- **Kathy Reichs**

  The American forensic anthropologist and best-selling novelist. To date, Kathy Reichs has written eleven novels based on real-life forensic science, and featuring her famous heroine, Temperance "Bones" Brennan.

- **Sir Bernard Spilsbury (1877–1947)**

  The leading British forensic pathologist in the first half of the 20th century. The cases he helped to solve include the notorious "brides in the bath" murders, and the Dr. Crippen murders.

Other topics to research

Bertillonism – Identifying people by measuring their head and body.

Body language – Reading clues in the way someone stands, sits, holds their arms, fidgets, and reacts when asked questions, and how the police use it to assess witnesses and suspects.

DNA databases – Are they a good thing? How would you feel if a sample of your DNA was taken and added to a database?

Electron microscope – Very powerful microscope used to examine the smallest particles.

Fingerprinting – Lots more to find out about the history of fingerprinting.

Low copy number DNA – Technique for producing DNA profiles from incredibly small samples.

The polygraph – The lie detector machine that can tell whether you're telling the truth.

Virtual autopsy – Examining a body using X-rays and body scanners, instead of cutting it open.

Voiceprint analysis – Way to identify people from the sound of their voices.

Find out more

Books (non-fiction)

Cool Careers: Crime Scene Investigator, Geoffrey M Horn
(Gareth Stevens Publishing, 2007)

Cool Science: Forensic Science, Ron Fridell (Lerner Publications, 2007)

Crimebusters: How Science Fights Crime, Clive Gifford
(Barron's Educational Series, 2007)

Crime Scene Investigation: Forensic Artist - Solving the Case with a Face,
Sue L Hamilton (ABDO & Daughters, 2008)

Crime Scene Investigation: DNA Analysis - Forensic Fluids & Follicles,
Sue L Hamilton (ABDO & Daughters, 2008)

Crime-Solving Science Experiments: Fingerprints, Kenneth G Rainis
(Enslow Publishers, 2006)

Books (fiction)

A Study in Scarlet, Sir Arthur Conan Doyle
First published in 1887, the first Conan Doyle novel to feature the Victorian
sleuth, Sherlock Holmes.

The Mysterious Affair at Styles, Agatha Christie
First published in 1920, the first Agatha Christie novel to feature the Belgian
detective, Hercule Poirot.

Deja Dead, Kathy Reichs
The first of more than 10 novels by real forensic anthropologist Kathy Reichs
to feature the fictional forensic anthropologist, Temperance Brennan.

Websites

http://library.thinkquest.org/04oct/00206/text_index.htm

Lots of information about forensic science from the ThinkQuest Library.

http://www.deathonline.net/decomposition/index.htm

A site from the Australian Museum that explains what happens to a human body after death.

http://www.sciencenewsforkids.org/articles/20041215/Feature1.asp

Learn more about a crime lab and what it does.

Organizations

Forensic Science Service
Trident Court
2920 Solihull Parkway
Birmingham Business Park
Birmingham B37 7YN
Website: www.forensic.gov.uk
One of the world's leading providers of forensic science and technology services, owned by the British government.

AFP Forensic Services
GPO Box 401
Canberra ACT 2601
Australia
Website: www.afp.gov.au/services/operational/forensics.html
Provides forensic science services to the Australian police.

Glossary

alpha radiation   particles with a positive electric charge given out by some radioactive substances

autopsy   examination of a dead body to find out the cause of death

beta radiation   electrons or positrons (electrons with a positive electric charge) given out by some radioactive substances

blood group   one of the types of blood humans can have. The main blood groups are A, B, AB, and O.

chemical reaction   process in which one substance is changed into a different substance

chromatography   scientific process for separating a mixture of chemicals from each other by passing them through a substance

chromosome   one of the structures inside the nucleus of a living cell that contain the genes

combustion   another word for burning, a chemical reaction in which a substance combines with oxygen and gives out light and heat

comparison microscope   scientific instrument that lets a forensic scientist see magnified views of two things, such as bullets, side by side

CSI   crime scene investigator

custody   held by police

database   set of information stored in a computer

DNA   deoxyribonucleic acid. DNA is the substance that genes are made of, and is found mainly in the nuclei of living cells.

DNA profile   pattern of the repeated sections of an individual's genetic code that can be used to identify the individual, also called a genetic fingerprint

electron   negatively charged particle in an atom

enzyme   one of the many proteins that help chemical reactions to happen in a living organism

evidence   items or facts used by crime investigators and courts to discover the truth

forensic   to do with the scientific investigation of crimes

forge   to copy or reproduce something (for instance, a bank note) and try to pass it off as the real thing

gamma rays radiation like light, but made of much shorter waves, shorter even than ultraviolet rays and X-rays. Gamma rays are given out by radioactive substances.

gene unit of inheritance carried on chromosomes in a cell nucleus

haemoglobin part of a red blood cell that absorbs oxygen and carries it around the body

inert inactive

infrared radiation like light but made of longer waves

luminol chemical substance that glows when it comes into contact with blood

magnetic field region of space where magnetic forces can be detected

mass spectrometer scientific instrument that separates a mixture of particles according to their mass

morgue place where bodies are stored until they can be buried or cremated, also called a mortuary

primer small explosive charge that sets off a larger charge

propellant substance that pushes something along, usually as a result of gases produced by combustion

radiation energy and particles given out by something, including light, heat, radio waves, and the particles and waves from radioactive substances

rifling grooves inside the barrel of a gun

serologist scientist who specializes in studying blood

spatter splashing. Blood spatter is the pattern made by blood that has splashed on a surface.

spectrophotometer scientific instrument for measuring the intensity of light at various wavelengths, or colours

suspect someone who is thought to have committed a crime

swab small piece of fibre (usually cotton wool) used to absorb fluids

ultraviolet radiation like light but made of shorter waves

X-rays radiation like light but made of much shorter waves. X-rays can pass through some substances and darken photographic film.

Index

− 3 DEC 2009